budgies . . .
in color

by ernest h. hart

completely illustrated with color photographs

Photography: Dr. Herbert R. Axelrod, Michael Gilroy, A. Jesse, Harry V. Lacey, Louise Van der Meid.

to Dom Golia, Jr.

Distributed in the UNITED STATES by T.F.H. Publications, Inc., One T.F.H. Plaza, Neptune City, NJ 07753; in CANADA to the Pet Trade by H & L Pet Supplies Inc., 27 Kingston Crescent, Kitchener, Ontario N2B 2T6; Rolf C. Hagen Ltd., 3225 Sartelon Street, Montreal 382 Quebec; in CANADA to the Book Trade by Macmillan of Canada (A Division of Canada Publishing Corporation), 164 Commander Boulevard, Agincourt, Ontario M1S 3C7; in ENGLAND by T.F.H. Publications, PO Box 15, Waterlooville PO7 6BQ; in AUSTRALIA AND THE SOUTH PACIFIC by T.F.H. (Australia) Pty. Ltd., Box 149, Brookvale 2100 N.S.W., Australia; in NEW ZEALAND by Ross Haines & Son, Ltd., 82 D Elizabeth Knox Place, Panmure, Auckland, New Zealand; in the PHILIPPINES by Bio-Research, 5 Lippay Street, San Lorenzo Village, Makati, Rizal; in SOUTH AFRICA by Multipet Pty. Ltd., P.O. Box 35347, Northway, 4065, South Africa. Published by T.F.H. Publications, Inc. Manufactured in the United States of America by T.F.H. Publications, Inc.

Contents

Budgerigars can make fine pets for people of all ages. They are quite affordable and their small size makes them easy to care for and easy to accommodate even in the smallest of apartments.

An opaline cobalt Budgie cock peeping out from his nestbox. If you are looking for a relatively trouble-free pet, a Budgie may be just the right choice for you.

1. Origin of the Budgie

The Budgie is a bird of as many names as colors . . . almost. The names we are most familiar with are Budgie, meaning Budgerigar, the native Australian name, and Parakeet. The scientific name for this most interesting of all birds is *Melopsittacus undulatus* and, to continue in the scientific vein for a moment, the Budgerigar is a warm-blooded vertebrate animal of the class Aves.

Other names used by writers and ornithologists are: Undulating Grass Parakeets (or Parrakeets, if you prefer), Shell Parrots, Warbling Grass Parakeets, Canary Parrots and Zebra Parakeets. The Budgie is the only living member of the genus *Melopsittacus undulatus* and the popular name by which it is called, Budgerigar, is a corruption of the word *"Betcherrygah"* used by the Australian Aborigine to differentiate this species of Parakeet from the many others that are native to the soil of the continent "down under." The native name means "pretty bird."

The Budgie, in the wild state, is native to Australia alone and lives in huge flocks on the large grass-covered plains feeding on the ripening grass seeds and nesting in the ancient, tall eucalyptus trees that reach their leafy arms up to the deep blue Australian sky. One single tree can house a multitude of breeding pairs of Budgies.

BUDGIE COLORS

The original wild Budgie was a green bird with a bright yellow face, black spots on the mask that adorns the face, and wavy black striations or bands, on the back, wings, and skull. The wild Budgie in Australia today is still the same color as it rises in clouds from the feeding places, a multitude blocking off the sun.

The domestic Budgie, those bred for pets or show birds, have departed from the basic green color and now come in many varieties of color and shades of those colors. The basic color of the bird, green, is composed of blue and yellow, a combination of colors that always makes green. *Mutations* occurred in the color genes of the Budgie. This means that the color genes, the very tiny parts of the body that control the bird's color, were changed or damaged. The first *mutation* occurred when the gene for blue refused to work in one or two of the domestic birds. The result was that the Budgie so affected was *yellow* instead of the ordinary green. Breeders used these first yellows to establish that color in the breed. Later the gene for yellow quit producing that color in a bird or two. The result was a *blue* bird. Breeders used these first *mutant blues* to produce the blue series.

As time passed many more *mutations* came into being, and breeders of Budgies used them to produce new color strains. Now the beautiful Budgie comes in three shades of blue and three shades of green, in violet, yellows, albinos (white in the blue series, lutino in the green series), all the many pastel shades of all these colors, grays, yellow-faced blues, white-wings, cinnamons (brown striations instead of black), greywings, opalines (a change in the body marking pattern), dominant and recessive pieds (splashes of white on the basic color), lacewings, fallows, crested, and dark-eyed clears. Combining several of these new color factors can produce the loveliest of birds. The beautiful "rainbow" Budgie is an example of this blending of several factors to produce a new color.

Of all the birds known to man none has shown the brilliant variety of mutant colors exhibited by the wonderful little former native of Australia that first came to us as a cage bird about 125 years ago.

2. Selecting the Budgie

When you go to your pet shop or a local Budgie breeder to buy a Budgie for a pet be sure you get a *young* one and be certain that it is a *male* Budgie. Young Budgies, particularly those just out of the nest, are the easiest to train.

A young Budgie has the black (or brown if it is cinnamon) striations extending up over the skull to the cere, which is the horny section over the Budgie's beak which contain the holes of the bird's nostrils. A young Budgie's feathers do not have the sheen or the deep distinct color that a grown bird has. The eyes are large and completely dark. Older birds have a ring of light color around the eye.

A singly kept Budgie will depend on you for companionship. If you feel that you don't have adequate time to spend with your pet, you might consider acquiring two birds, who can keep each other company.

A natural tree branch can make a good perch for your Budgie, as its variations in thickness promote good exercising of the bird's toes. Be sure, however, that any natural perching devices have not been chemically treated.

It is not easy for the novice to differentiate between the sexes in young Budgies. The male bird makes the best pet so you must be sure and select a male. To do so look at the cere, that section of horny substance over the beak. In a very young Budgie the male will exhibit a pink cere, so pink, in fact, that it almost appears to be sore. The female youngster will show a very pale blue cere, almost white. As they grow older, the male's cere becomes a bright blue, and the female's cere turns from blue to a creamy white to tan and finally, when in breeding shape, to dark brown.

Breeders and other knowledgeable persons, can often sex Budgies by the shape of their heads, the male's head being bigger and rounder with more backskull, the female's head appearing higher in front and dropping back in a greater slant toward the back.

Select a lively bird that is alert and unafraid. Avoid the bird that sits on the perch with its feathers all puffed up and eyes half closed. Make sure the young Budgie has learned to eat seeds, either on the floor of the cage or in the containers provided for them. Young birds are fed by their parents and there is a time between parent feeding and adequately providing for themselves when they must learn to crack and eat seeds which have been provided for them by the breeder.

3. Housing the Pet Budgie

In the pet shop you will find two basically different kinds of bird cages. One is for *canaries* and the other is for *Budgies*. Don't make the mistake of buying a canary cage for a Budgie.

You will notice that certain cages will have rods that gradually slope together as though gathered, getting narrower as they merge at the top, generally in the area where the hanging ring or swing can be found. This is a canary cage and *not* for Budgies. Your Budgie is a curious and lively little bird and will quite possibly push his head between the bars and move upward toward the apex of the cage and the narrowing bars will choke him before he can pull free.

Budgie cages have open containers for seeds and water and they are located inside the cage. Canary food containers are hooded and clipped to the outside of the cage so that the bird has to put his head through an opening in the bars to feed. Budgies dislike doing this. They want *open* containers that are easily accessible. Make sure your Budgie has a swing in his cage and one or two of the many toys available for these curious and intelligent little beauties to play with. Do not jam up the cage with toys. Allow plenty of space for the bird to fly and play in.

At night, when you go to bed, cover your Budgie's cage. He will sleep better and not chatter in the morning until you remove the cover and greet him with a sprightly "Good morning."

4. Feeding the Budgie

Like all birds, the Budgie has a higher body temperature than that of other animals, and his breathing rate is faster. These peculiarities are an index of the intense activity of a bird's life, flying vigorously and, in the case of the wild Budgie, migrating from one feeding ground to the next. Also, Budgies do not have teeth with which to grind their food, they possess large crops for secreting crop milk to feed their young, and like all birds that feed primarily on grains and seeds, the glandular part of the stomach is small. We must take all these elements into consideration when we feed our Budgies.

Your Budgie will be completely dependent upon you to provide him with a healthy diet that will meet his nutritional requirements. Pet shops stock a wide variety of foods specially formulated for Budgerigars.

For the terrific energy which must be engendered for flying, the Budgie needs *carbohydrates*, and this food element is supplied generously in seeds and grains. The commercial mixes of Budgie seeds composed of *canary seed, millet seed* and some *oats* provide your Budgie with the carbohydrates he needs and some of the fat he also needs through the oats. Canary seeds are easier to shuck (which the Budgie does to get at the kernel or meat of the seed), and therefore should be supplied in greater volume in the mix when you are feeding a young or baby Budgie.

The white object attached to the side of this Budgie's cage is a *cuttlebone*. This dietary supplement is an excellent source of minerals for your pet.

Not having any teeth the Budgie needs some artificial aid in grinding his food for digestion. This you supply him through the *grit* you buy. The grit is eaten by your Budgie and, in the gizzard, grinds the food to digestive consistency. Good grit contains necessary vitamins and minerals for your Budgie, too. *Cuttlebone*, or the commercial *calcium blocks*, should also be given your bird because they supply him with calcium and phosphorus and help exercise his beak.

Your Budgie needs *cellulose* (which he discards when he shucks his seeds), and it can be supplied him through vegetable greens and a piece of fresh tree bark or wood. Remember to always wash and rinse any greens and be sure that any tree bark or buds you may give your Budgie has *not* been sprayed. Supply water generously, though if you feed fresh wet greens, your Budgie will get most

13

of his water supply from them. Alfalfa, clover, chick-weed, dandelion, lawn clippings, seeding grasses, fruit tree buds on the branch, carrots, corn and fresh fruits, are all good for your Budgie.

Commercial supplements can also be fed to, and enjoyed by, your Budgie. Be careful that you do not feed too much and your bird becomes over-fat.

Generally Budgies do not like to take baths as do canaries. Give your Budgie a wet lettuce leaf or wet greens, put at the bottom of his cage, and he will roll in it with great vigor and enjoyment, fluffing out his feathers and keeping clean in this manner.

5. Budgie Management

Clean, well-cared-for-Budgies are most often healthy Budgies, free from parasitic invaders and the small ills that bring greater woes in their wake.

Cleanliness is the first essential of good management.

When handling your Budgie, do so in a calm and gentle manner. The more time you spend with your bird, the sooner he will become accustomed to your presence.

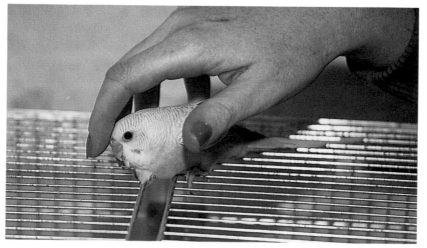

Remove all unconsumed green food from the cage every day and keep the floor of the cage covered with a piece of paper that you can trim to an exact fit with a scissors. By removing this piece of paper and daily replacing it with a fresh piece, you will keep the floor of the cage clean. Many Budgies will chew up the paper and leave holes and unsightly, chewed bits of paper on the cage floor. If this bothers you, replace the paper with a layer of clean sand on the floor. The tray that the floor is made of can be removed, the sand dumped out, the tray cleaned, and a new sand surface put on the floor.

A small paint scraper is a handy tool for scraping the cage floor and freeing it of accumulated droppings and debris. Once a week all food pots, water troughs and tubes, should be washed in hot water to which has been added soap, soda, or detergent. Allow these items to soak a bit, then wash them and very thoroughly rinse them.

Once a week spray your Budgie with a good parasitic spray (there are many on the market), a liquid made especially for Budgies that contains no toxic ingredients harmful to the bird.

While indulging in this weekly cleaning chore, also remove the perches from the cage (don't forget the swing perch), and clean them by quickly scraping with the paint scraper and then rolling a piece of sandpaper around them and running them in and out of the sandpaper a few times.

When your Budgie moults some of the downy feathers will even adhere to the cage bars. To clean away moulted feathers, a most useful tool is the tube attachment of your vacuum cleaner. First, though, get your bird used to this implement so he will not be frightened, then use it to suck up all those light and hard-to-get feathers he has cast in the moult.

Keep your Budgie and his quarters clean and you will keep him healthy.

Adequate perching space is important to your Budgie's well-being. Additionally, make sure perches are kept clean.

Locate your Budgie's cage in an area that is well ventilated and free from drafts. Be mindful that drastic changes in the temperature of the bird's environment must be avoided.

6. Training Your Budgie

Training the Budgie as a pet is not a difficult job. Your task will be much easier if (as I recommended earlier) you acquire a very young chick, one that has been out of the nest box only a few days but is cracking seeds and eating without any trouble. Most youngsters of this age will almost immediately become finger tame, the *first* step in training the pet bird. They are so young that they have not yet learned to be afraid.

Give the little Budgie a couple of days to get settled in his new cage and become accustomed to his new environment. Throw some seeds on the floor of his cage until you are sure that he is eating from the regular seed cups. When you give him seeds or water, or are working around his cage, speak to him in a quiet, soothing tone and make sure that your movements are slow and deliberate and not designed to startle him. Try to always keep your hands at a level with, or lower than, the bird, for Budgies are afraid of movements above or over their heads.

FINGER TRAINING

Once your Budgie has settled into his new quarters (about the second day after bringing him home), begin his finger training. Wait until he is on the perch, then gently and slowly insert your hand into the cage through the cage door, and slowly move your fingers toward the bird, meanwhile speaking soothingly and coaxingly. Stroke his breast very gently with your finger, repeating the name you have chosen for him over and over again. Frequently the bird will immediately hop upon your finger. If he doesn't, if he hops down from the perch, let your hand remain inside the cage without movement until he returns to the perch, then repeat the whole maneuver again.

Budgies are gregarious birds, occupying most of their time with one another. When kept too long in isolation, a Budgerigar can die with no apparent signs of physical illness.

If he remains on the perch but doesn't step onto your finger, press your index finger (back of the finger, palm out and away from the bird) gently against the lower breast where the Budgie's thigh joins the body. This pressure will put him slightly off balance, and he will step onto your finger of necessity. When he does command him gently to *"Up,"* or *"Finger."* After a few tries he will be conditioned to step up on your finger as soon as it is presented to him in his cage and you issue the command *"Up."*

The next step is to remove him from the cage while he is on your finger. Remember to move your hand slowly. It is best to try this exercise first at night, for he may become frightened and fly from your hand and hurt himself. But, if it is night and he flies from your hand, mark the spot where he flew to, turn off the lights and, by

Patience and consistency are important elements in successfully taming and training your Budgie. Once your pet has been tamed, it will come to enjoy the attention it receives from you during training sessions.

A lovely lutino Budgie. Budgerigars are available in a striking variety of colors.

turning the beams of a flashlight on and off quickly to locate him, you can walk up and capture him easily and return him to his cage.

It won't be long before he will perch on your finger and you can remove him from the cage. He will probably fly around a bit and then return to your finger if you hold it up and give him his command. Soon he will also be perching on your shoulder or head as you work around the house. It is a good idea to purchase a long, perch-size round stick (dowel, in hardware or lumber companies) which you can hold out to him if he is in a high spot which you can't reach when you wish to bring him down.

CLIPPING OF WINGS

Many trainers advocate clipping some of the long flight feathers off the wings so that the bird cannot fly and will therefore (they claim) become finger trained more quickly. Except for the occasional Budgie who constantly flies away when taken from his cage, and will not mind your commands, I do not think that clipping of the wings is at all necessary.

It is best to cage your Budgie at meal time. Budgies

Clipping the wings (to prevent a bird from flying) is a matter of personal choice on the part of the owner. This procedure requires knowledge of the bird's wing structure *and* a steady hand.

It is recommended that you cover your Budgie's cage when you go to bed at night: doing so will ensure that the bird gets sufficient and restful sleep.

are very inquisitive. He will like to be close to you and will fly onto the table to examine everything, chat with his reflection in the silverware, and steal tiny scraps from your plate. But a Budgie plopping into a plate of hot soup can become a quick and painful case for a veterinarian. Or, a pet jumping onto your head from his former position in the middle of a piece of chocolate cream pie, when your involuntary scream frightens him, can wreak havoc with the most carefully done coiffure.

A playpen for your pet, furnished with an assortment of the colorful toys made specifically for Budgies, can provide both you and your pet with hours of fun. Your Budgie will learn many cute tricks by himself when allowed freedom in a pen with an assortment of interesting objects.

This Budgie is fascinated by his own reflection. If you are going to permit your pet to fly about freely in a room, you should be present to keep a watchful eye on him.

Most Budgie fanciers would agree that a young Budgie—as opposed to a mature one—is a better candidate for a training program.

7. Teaching Your Budgie to Talk

All it takes is time and patience to teach your Budgie to talk. Remember, he does not recognize words, or words in sequence; he merely recognizes sound and has the ability to reproduce those sounds he hears in sequence. He *will* learn that certain sounds produce certain results and is smart enough to eventually use those sounds to get specific results.

Repetition is the basis of successfully teaching a Budgie to speak. Begin with easy sounds, the bird's name and a word or two, such as: "*Hello, Petey!*" Repeat this over and over again, always in the same tone and at the same speed. Make sure you are alone and with nothing to distract the bird. The Budgie learns more quickly when the voice used to train him is in the higher registers. Women, therefore, find more success in teaching such feathered pupils than do men.

You must be extremely patient. Repeat the phrase you wish your Budgie to learn over and over again, even though it seems futile because the bird doesn't utter a sound that could be even loosely interpreted as being close to the simple words you wish him to repeat. Sometimes it is weeks, in some rare cases even months, before the bird begins to make strange sounds that are different than the normal Budgie chatter. Soon after this the Budgie will begin to repeat the words you have been teaching him, generally mixed in with a lot of other garbled sounds. Once your Budgie learns a few words and will repeat them clearly, he will begin to learn more quickly until he becomes a veritable chatterbox. He will even pick up and repeat words that have not been deliberately taught to him. The author has heard birds repeat nursery rhymes, mimic other animals, trains, etc., even tell jokes and whistle and sing songs.

8. Treating the Sick Budgie

When your Budgie becomes ill he generally sits puffed up on the perch and *looks* like a sick bird. He doesn't eat as well as he should or he fails to eat at all, and his droppings change in appearance and become watery, or green, or both. Frequently there will be a discharge from the eyes or nostrils and the eyes will be half closed.

The first thing to do, and do at once, is to provide *heat*. A temperature of 85 degrees fahrenheit is in order immediately. Drape three sides of the cage with cloth and place an electric lamp on the fourth side so that the heat is contained within the cage. Hospital cages are made for large aviaries. They are enclosed and have a false bottom in which bulbs create the heat necessary to help the sick bird.

If you have a small hot water bottle, put it on the bottom of the cage with a cloth cover. If the bird is eating, a little sugar or honey mixed with the food will aid in its recovery. One of the medications that contain antibiotics and can be purchased at your pet shop, can be used. Liquid medicine, if administered to the bird with an eye-dropper, should be carefully handled. A drop at a time should be given or the bird may choke.

Budgies are susceptible to respiratory diseases. Wheezing is one of the specific symptoms along with the others already mentioned. Heat is one of the great curealls for Budgies and will generally bring your Budgie back to health unless he is really very sick. If he is, then it is best to bring him to your veterinarian for treatment.

27

The more familiar you are with your pet's behavior, the easier it will be for you to discern when he is not feeling well.

The best ways to prevent illness are to feed your Budgie a nutritious diet and to keep his surroundings and equipment clean and free of germs and parasites.

Budgies are generally very hardy little birds and if you care for yours well, always keep seeds and water available, and keep your Budgie clean and comfortable, you will find, as so many others have, that you own the finest, and probably the most beautiful, pet in the world.

9. Bird Shows

There are many bird shows held in various parts of the country. The fall shows start in October and continue into December. Baby shows are held by many clubs in June or July. Most all of the shows are sponsored by local Budgerigar clubs under the auspices of either the American Budgerigar Society, or the United Budgerigar Society.

There is a standard of perfection used in judging Budgies. A perfect bird would be entitled to a score of

Pet quality or show quality, Budgies are charming little birds that will win your heart with their endearing ways.

100, but the perfect bird has yet to be bred and shown. The various parts of the bird are rated, percentage wise, according to their importance in the specific color or pattern phase being judged. Some shows bench as many as a thousand birds, with classes for all the different colors, young and old birds in various show categories. Beautiful trophies, ribbons and rosettes are awarded the winning birds and the shows are generally quite interesting and exciting.

If you are interested in Budgies a day spent at one of the large Budgie shows in or close to your locale, will be very much worthwhile. Most pet shops have schedules of the shows.

Given the proper attention and care, a Budgie can provide you with years of pleasure and companionship.

Attractive and hardy, Budgerigars are one of the world's favorite cage birds.